Poe

UNRIDDLING

UNRIDDLING

All Sorts of Riddles
to Puzzle Your Guessery

COLLECTED FROM AMERICAN FOLKLORE
by Alvin Schwartz

drawings by Sue Truesdell

A Harper Trophy Book
Harper & Row, Publishers

Unriddling

Text copyright © 1983 by Alvin Schwartz
Illustrations copyright © 1983 by Susan G. Truesdell

First Harper Trophy edition, 1987.
Published in hardcover by J. B. Lippincott, New York.

LIBRARY OF CONGRESS CATALOGING IN PUBLICATION DATA
Schwartz, Alvin, date.
   Unriddling: all sorts of riddles to puzzle your
guessery.

   Bibliography: p.
   Summary: A collection of riddles of various traditional
types including queer-word, hidden-answer, neck, leg,
rebus, and tricky-question riddles.
   1. Riddles, Juvenile.   [1. Riddles.   2. Folklore—
United States]   I. Truesdell, Susan G., ill.   II. Title.
PN6371.5.S384 1983   818′.5402′08   82-48778
ISBN 0-397-32029-9
ISBN 0-397-32030-2 (lib. bdg.)

   (A Harper Trophy Book)
ISBN 0-06-446057-6 (pbk.)

Also by Alvin Schwartz

CHIN MUSIC:
Tall Talk and Other Talk

CROSS YOUR FINGERS, SPIT IN YOUR HAT:
Superstitions and Other Beliefs

FLAPDOODLE:
Pure Nonsense from American Folklore

KICKLE SNIFTERS
AND OTHER FEARSOME CRITTERS

SCARY STORIES TO TELL IN THE DARK

TOMFOOLERY:
Trickery and Foolery with Words

A TWISTER OF TWISTS,
A TANGLER OF TONGUES

WHEN I GREW UP LONG AGO

WHOPPERS:
Tall Tales and Other Lies

WITCRACKS:
Jokes and Jests from American Folklore

I CAN READ Books®
(for younger readers)

BUSY BUZZING BUMBLEBEES
AND OTHER TONGUE TWISTERS

IN A DARK, DARK ROOM
AND OTHER SCARY STORIES

TEN COPYCATS IN A BOAT
AND OTHER RIDDLES

THERE IS A CARROT IN MY EAR
AND OTHER NOODLE TALES

Contents

Contents

Strengthening for the Brain

What is black and white and yellow? You probably know the answer to this riddle joke already. If you don't, you will find it in Chapter 2. Riddles of this kind are the most popular ones we have today.

When your great-grandparents were growing up, they had all sorts of riddles we no longer use. There were queer-word riddles, hidden-answer riddles, neck riddles, leg riddles, rebus riddles, tricky-question riddles, and other types you will find in this book.

In those days people spent quite a bit of time at riddling and unriddling, at asking riddles and trying to solve them. It not only was fun. It was "strengthening for the brain," they said. It stretched your mind and sharpened your wits. As a joke, some said there was a special part of the brain that figured out the answers to riddles. They called it the "guessery."

In the evenings after supper, often the elders in a family would ask the riddles they had learned when they were young, and the young people would try to answer them. Then the young people might give their riddles. Spending an evening this way was a tradition in many countries.

People have been riddling and unriddling for as long as anyone knows. One of the most ancient riddles we have is more than six thousand years old. It was found in the city of Babylon carved in a stone tablet that was used in a school. "What grows fat without eating?" the riddle asked the schoolchildren in those days. The answer: "A rain cloud."

After all these years, we still have great fun with riddles. We enjoy the same things about them that people always have enjoyed. One is asking a riddle that no one else can solve. Another is solving a riddle that no one else can answer. Let us see how many riddles you can answer in the pages ahead.

ALVIN SCHWARTZ

UNRIDDLING

—1—
No Way Out

A girl was locked up in a metal room. Never mind how she got there. Her problem was how to get out. There was a door in that room, but there was no key to the door. And there were no windows in the room or other openings.

The only furniture was a piano and a wooden table. There was a saw on the table, and a baseball bat in the corner. Other than that the room was empty.

The girl thought and thought. Finally she figured out how to escape. She was so smart she figured out *four* different ways. What did she do? Take your choice.

SOLUTIONS

1. With the saw, she cut the table in half. Since two halves make a whole, she crawled out through the hole.

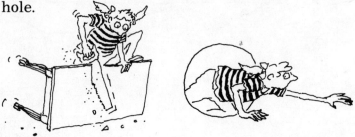

2. She played the piano until she found the right key. Then she unlocked the door and let herself out.

3. She swung the baseball bat three times. It was three strikes, and she was out.

4. She ran around and around the room until she wore herself out.

When at last she was free, she shouted for joy. She shouted so long and so loud her throat became a little hoarse. Then she got on that horse and rode away.

— 2 —
Riddle Jokes

These riddle jokes have answers you never would expect, and each is as silly as can be.

1. What has four legs and goes "Oom! oom!"?

2. What has eighteen legs and red spots and catches flies?

3. What is black and white and yellow?

4. What is white on the outside, green on the inside, and hops?

5. What does a six-hundred-pound gorilla eat?

6. What has six eyes and cannot see?

7. What does the ear hear?

8. How does a witch tell time?

9. Why does a giraffe need such a long neck?

10. What do you get when you cross a bee with a bell?

SOLUTIONS

1. A cow walking backward.

2. A baseball team with measles.

3. A cowardly zebra.

4. A frog sandwich.

5. Anything he wants.

6. Three blind mice.

7. Only the nose knows.

8. With a witch watch.

9. Because its head is so far from its body.

10. A humdinger.

3

Strange Happenings

Each of these riddles is about something strange and puzzling that needs to be explained.

1. The Elevator

Richard and his parents live on the tenth floor of an apartment house. Each morning Richard rides down to the lobby in the elevator. Then he walks to school. When he returns home in the afternoon, he takes the elevator to the third floor. Then he walks up the rest of the way. Why does Richard get off at the third floor instead of the tenth floor?

2. The Telltale Puddle

When George and Rachel were found, they both were dead. They were lying in a puddle of water. There was broken glass all around them. What had happened?

3. *The Race to Mecca*

A rich Arab died. In his will he asked that his two sons race one another on horseback. They were to race to Mecca, twenty miles away. The one whose horse finished *last* would inherit all of his father's wealth.

The day of the race, the two brothers rode their horses as slowly as they could. But when night came, they had covered only a mile. At that rate, the race would take three weeks, and they could not spare all that time.

They spent that night at an inn. When they told the innkeeper about their problem, he thought for a minute. Then he gave them two words of advice, which they decided to follow.

Early the next morning they rode off toward Mecca. But now they rode as fast as the horses would carry them. What was the advice that the innkeeper gave them?

4. Two Masked Men
A man left home one night. He turned to the right and started running. He ran straight ahead. Then he turned to the left. After a while he turned to the left again. He was running faster than ever. Then he turned to the left once more and headed for home. But in the distance he saw two masked men waiting for him. Who were they?

5. The Hundred-Dollar Bill
A wealthy man named Richard Ellis had been counting his money. When he finished, he accidentally left a hundred-dollar bill on his desk. But when he returned for it a short while later, it was gone. Only two

other persons could have seen the bill. One was the maid. The other was the butler.

The maid told him that she had hidden it for safe-keeping under a green book that was on the desk. But when they looked, the bill was not there.

The butler said he had found the bill where the maid had left it. He had placed it inside the book, where he thought there was less chance that some-body would find it. He had written down the page numbers so that he would not forget them. The bill was between pages 35 and 36, he said. But when they looked, there was no money in the book.

After Mr. Ellis had talked to the maid and the butler, he called the police. He was sure he knew who had taken the money. Who was it?

6. *Two Trails in the Jungle*

A scientist was searching for a tribe that lived in the jungle. Members of this tribe always told the truth. There was another tribe nearby that spoke the same language as the first tribe and wore the same kind of clothing. It was impossible for an outsider to tell them apart, except for one thing: Members of the second tribe never told the truth.

The scientist came to a place where the trail he was following became two trails. One led to the truth tellers and the other led to the liars. But he did not know which was which.

As he tried to decide, a man came out of the jungle. The scientist could not tell whether the man was a truth teller or a liar, but he asked him a question. Based on the man's answer, he chose the correct trail, the one that led to the truth tellers. What did the scientist ask him, and what was the man's reply?

SOLUTIONS

1. Richard was too short to reach the button for the tenth floor. The button for the third floor was as high as he could reach.

2. George and Rachel were goldfish. They died when their fishbowl fell to the floor and broke.

3. The innkeeper's advice was to "swap horses." The old Arab had said that the son whose horse finished last would inherit his riches. But he did

not say that his sons had to ride the horses they owned. When they exchanged horses, the son whose horse finished last still inherited his father's wealth, even though the horse he was riding came in first.

4. The man who was running was a baseball player. He had just hit a triple and was trying to turn it into a home run. One of the masked men waiting for him at home plate was the other team's catcher. The other masked man was the umpire.

5. The butler stole the money. He did not tell the truth when he said that he had placed the hundred-dollar bill between pages 35 and 36. In a book, these pages are printed on opposite sides of the same sheet of paper.

6. The scientist asked, "Which trail do I take to get to your village?" If the man was a truth teller, he would have pointed to the trail the scientist wanted. If he was a liar, he would *not* have pointed to the trail that led to his village. He also would have pointed to the trail that led to the truth tellers.

4
Tricky Questions

These seem like ordinary, run-of-the-mill riddles, but watch out. Each of them has a trick or a catch to it.

1. Which is heavier, a full moon or a half moon?

2. Which word with five letters becomes shorter when you add two letters?

3. How can you get ten horses into nine stalls in a barn? P.S. You can't squeeze two horses into one stall.

4. If you have two shoes and just one sock, what do you need?

5. Which is right, "Six and five *are* thirteen?" or "Six and five *is* thirteen?"

6. What can you never eat for breakfast?

7.   "England, Ireland, Scotland, Wales,
       Monkeys, rats, and wiggletails."
       Spell that with only four letters.

8. You have two coins that add up to fifty-five cents. If one is not a nickel, what are they?

9. Which has more legs, one cow or no cow?

10. A hungry donkey was tied to a rope eight feet long. About thirty feet away there was a pile of fresh carrots. The donkey badly wanted those carrots. How did he reach them?

11. How many donkeys' tails would it take to reach from the earth to the moon?

12. How would you divide nine apples equally among ten children?

SOLUTIONS

1. A full moon is lighter. So a half moon must be heavier.

2. The word "short."

3. T E N H O R S E S

4. Another sock. If a friend gives this answer, ask if *that* is what he or she really wants.

5. Neither is correct. Six and five are eleven, not thirteen.

6. Lunch and dinner.

7. T-h-a-t.

8. One coin is a fifty-cent piece. The *other* is a nickel.

9. One cow has four legs. No cow has more legs than that.

10. The other end of the rope was not tied to anything. The donkey just walked over to the carrots, dragging the rope behind him.

11. Just one, if it is long enough. A similar riddle appeared in a riddle collection printed in England in 1511. It read, "How many calues [calves'] tayles behoueth [would it take] to reche [reach] frome the erthe to the skye?" The answer: "No more but one, an it be longe ynough."

12. By making applesauce.

5

Droodles

A droodle is a picture riddle. To solve a droodle, you must figure out what the picture stands for. Usually it is some ordinary object like a used lollipop stick or a fried egg. But it is always shown from an unusual angle, and that makes it hard to identify. This is a droodle:

It is, of course, a giraffe passing by a window.

Picture riddles like these are very old. Artists in Italy were creating them in the seventeenth century, and possibly earlier. But they were not silly as droodles are today. This is one of those early drawings.

It shows a blind beggar coming around a corner. In the drawing only his cup, in which people placed coins, and his stick can be seen.

It was not until the 1950s that picture riddles became known as droodles. The name "droodle" is a combination of the words "drawing" and "doodle." They were given that name by Roger Price, who compiled several books of droodles.

Let's see how good you are at solving some others. Study each of them for a few minutes, then decide.

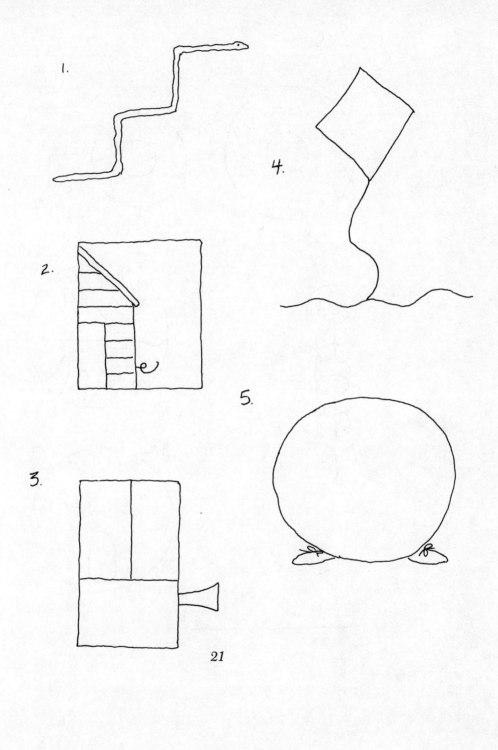

1.

2.

3.

4.

5.

6.

7.

9.

10.

8.

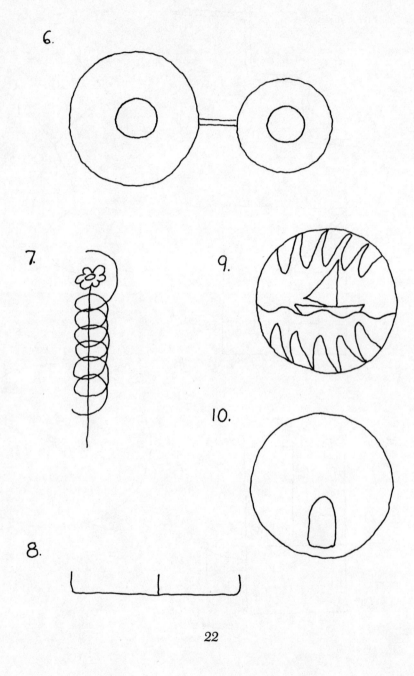

22

SOLUTIONS

1. A snake going upstairs.

2. A pig hiding behind a barn.

3. A small boy in a telephone booth blowing a horn.

4. A man aboard a submarine flying a kite.

5. A bubble-blowing champion.

6. A man in a sombrero frying an egg in a skillet, as seen from above.

7. A flower in the spring.

8. A hair comb with only one tooth left.

9. Looking out from inside a shark.

10. View from the bottom of a soda-pop can.

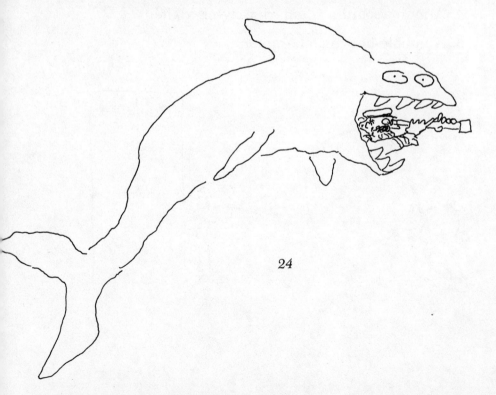

— 6 —

What Does GHOTI Really *Spell?*

What does G H O T I *really* spell?

To find out, pronounce GH as in "tou*gh*,"
                  O as in "w*o*men," and
                TI as in "emo*ti*on."

SOLUTION

When you pronounce GH as *ff*,
O as *ih*, and
TI as *sh*,
GHOTI really spells
FISH!

7

I'm My Own Grandpaw

At one time almost everybody had a large family. Along with mothers, fathers, sisters, and brothers, there were aunts, uncles, cousins, nieces, nephews, grandmothers, and grandfathers, and also fathers-in-law, mothers-in-law, sisters-in-law, brothers-in-law, and more.

Often there were so many relatives, it was hard to figure out how each was related to all of the others. In one family things got so complicated that a man turned out to be his own grandpaw. At least that is what a popular song said. To learn how this could happen, see page 99.

To solve the riddles in this chapter, you must decide how certain people are related to one another. If you make believe that they are all part of your family, it will seem less complicated.

1. Your grandmother has four daughters. Three of them are your aunts. Who is the fourth one?

2. If your uncle's sister is not your aunt, who is she?

3. Who is your sister's husband's mother-in-law?

4. Who is your mother's brother's brother-in-law?

5. If Dick's father is Tom's son, how is Dick related to Tom?

6. A beggar's brother died, but the man who died had no brother. How could that be?

7. A man went to the hospital to visit a sick relative. He was asked whom he wanted to see, and he replied:

   "Brothers and sisters I have none,
   But that boy's father is my father's son."

   Who was that?

8. And who is this?

   It is not my sister and not my brother,
   But it is a child of my father and mother.

SOLUTIONS

1. Your mother.

2. Your mother.

3. Your mother.

4. Your father.

5. Dick is Tom's grandson. A similar riddle was in use in the United States in the 1770s.

6. He had a sister who was a beggar.

7. The man had come to visit his son.

8. It is you!

— 8 —
Elephant Riddles

The elephant riddles in this chapter first appeared in the 1960s, along with hundreds of others. They asked all sorts of questions about elephants, including these:

1. How do you talk to an elephant?

2. How do you get down off an elephant?

3. How do you capture an elephant?

4. How do you make an elephant float?

5. How do you make a statue of an elephant?

6. What is the difference between an elephant and a flea?

SOLUTIONS

1. Use big words.

2. You don't. You get down off a goose or a duck.

3. To capture an elephant:
   - Put up a sign that says

     WATER FOR ELFANTS

     When an elephant sees how you spelled "elephant," it will start laughing.
   - While it is laughing, look at it through the wrong end of a telescope or a pair of binoculars. That will make it very small.
   - Pick up the elephant with a pair of tweezers and drop it in a jar.

4. To make an elephant float, add two scoops of ice cream and one elephant to a quart of root beer.

5. Get a big piece of stone. Cut away everything that does not look like an elephant.

6. An elephant can have fleas, but a flea cannot have elephants.

— 9 —

Who Am I? What Am I?

These riddles are about people, animals, and other things. Each has enough clues to lead you to the right answer.

1. Only My Family Loves Me
I am no bigger than a house cat. But no house cat am I. Dressed in black and white, I steal through the dark raiding vegetable gardens and garbage pails for food. Although I am gentle and rather good-looking, only my family loves me. Everyone else avoids me. If they see me, they run.

2. Nothing Can Change Me
I have eyes, but I see nothing. I have ears, but I hear

nothing. I have a mouth, but I cannot speak. I always will look just as I look now. If I am young, I will stay young. If I am old, I will remain old. Nothing can change me.

3. My Great Adventure

I may have the face of a great man or a great woman. When I am very young, I make my first and only journey. The day I set out, I am bright and colorful and look my very best. I travel from one city to another, or from one country to another. I may go halfway around the world to reach my destination. This trip is my great adventure, but within a few days or weeks it is over. By the time I arrive, I no longer am very attractive. My face is smudged with dirt and ink, and usually I am thrown away without a second glance.

4. Everyone Needs My Help

I dig out tiny caves and store gold and silver in them. I also build bridges of silver and make crowns of gold. They are the smallest you could imagine. Sooner or later everybody needs my help. Yet many people are afraid to let me help them.

5. I Cannot Keep Still

I have a head, but I do not have eyes or ears. I foam at the mouth, but I never bite. I roar, but I have no tongue. I lie in a bed, but I have no back. I rise, I fall, I rush and run, but I have neither legs nor feet. I was born in the mountains, but I go down to the ocean whenever I can. I cannot keep still for a moment. I am as restless as can be.

6. Without Me Nothing Can Be Done

Of all the things in the world, I am the shortest and the longest, the swiftest and the slowest. I am the thing people waste the most. Yet they need me more than anything else, for without me nothing can be done.

SOLUTIONS

1. A skunk.

2. A painting or a photograph of someone.

3. A postage stamp.

4. A dentist.

5. A river.

6. Time.

—10—
A Punctuation Riddle

You may think that this riddle tale is filled with lies. But the old woodsman who told the story told the truth. It is the punctuation that mixed things up. You can make sense out of his tale, and solve the riddle, without changing a single word. Just change the punctuation.

"I saw some wood floating in the air;
I saw a skylark bigger than a bear;
I saw an elephant waving its hands;
I saw a baby breaking iron bands;
I saw a blacksmith weighing half a ton;
I saw a statue having a lot of fun;
I saw a schoolboy nearly ten feet tall;
I saw an oak tree spanning Niagara Falls;
I saw a rainbow black and white and brown;
I saw a parasol walking through town;
I saw a postman, and I saw some wood."

SOLUTION

"I saw some wood;
   floating in the air, I saw a skylark;
   bigger than a bear, I saw an elephant;
   waving its hands, I saw a baby;
   breaking iron bands, I saw a blacksmith;
   weighing half a ton, I saw a statue;
   having a lot of fun, I saw a schoolboy;
   nearly ten feet tall, I saw an oak tree;
   spanning Niagara Falls, I saw a rainbow;
   black and white and brown, I saw a parasol;
   walking through town, I saw a postman;
   and I saw some wood."

— 11 —
Rebus Riddles

A rebus is a riddle in which pictures, letters, and numbers stand for words. This is an example of a rebus:

The rebus riddles in this chapter look like simple equations. But to solve them, you add and subtract letters, not numbers. Here is one such an equation: RAT − T + DISH = ?

Here is how to solve it.

1. The first picture shows a rat. On a piece of paper, print R-A-T.

2. Now subtract the letter T from R-A-T. That leaves R-A.

3. The second picture shows a dish. To R-A add D-I-S-H, and you have the answer. It is RADISH!

Try these rebus riddles. In each, the solution is the name of an animal, a bird, or a city.

1.  − Y + 🌙 − M = ?

2. 🥫 − N + 🍈 + E − 1 = ?

3. 🚕 + 👂 − 🐻 + 🛒 − 🚗 = ?

4. 🪑 + 🐄🐄🐄 − 🐱 = ?

5. 👨 − N + 🗄 − E + O = ?

6.

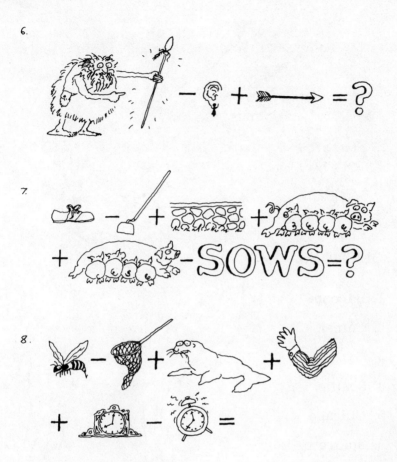

7.

8.

The last two riddles are only a picture and a letter. The answer to Number 9 is the name of a bird. The answer to Number 10 is a name shared by several cities and a supersonic airliner.

9.

10.

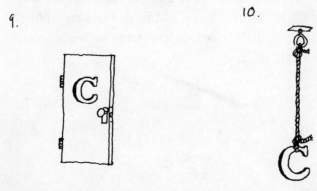

SOLUTIONS.

1. Baboon.

2. Camel.

3. Cat.

4. Seattle.

5. Chicago.

6. Sparrow.

7. Swallow.

8. Horse.

9. Condor, from C on door.

10. Concord, from C on cord: the city or town of Concord, New Hampshire, Massachusetts, North Carolina, and California; the Concorde, a supersonic airliner.

—12—

What Never Was and Never Will Be?

What never was and never will be?

SOLUTION.

A mouse's nest in a cat's ear.

—13—
Letter Riddles

Each of the first three riddles is about one word and the letters in that word. But beware of the fourth riddle. The answer is a trick!

1. I have seven letters.
   The first two stand for a boy.
   The first three stand for a girl.
   The first four stand for a brave boy.
   But all my letters stand for a brave girl.
   What word am I?

2. I have four letters.
    I am something a fisherman needs
      when fishing in deep waters.
    But remove my first letter,
      and I become food for a horse.
    Now return my first letter
      and remove my last letter,
      and I am a well-known snake.
    In each case, what word am I?

3. I have five letters.
    I describe something that contains nothing.
    Remove my first letter,
      and I sound the same.
    Remove my last letter,
      and I sound no different.
    Take away my middle letter,
      and you still will know me.
    What word am I?

4. Remove my first letter,
      and I do not change.
    Remove my second letter,
      and I do not change.
    Remove all of my letters,
      and I am still the same.
    Who am I?

SOLUTIONS

1. He, her, hero, heroine.

2. Boat, oat, boa.

3. Empty, mpty, mpt, mt.

4. A postman.

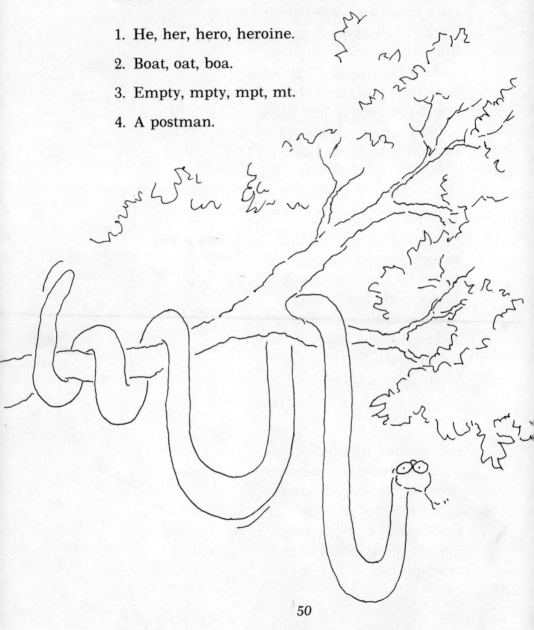

——14——
Crossing the River

This kind of riddle goes back more than a thousand years. In those days monks in isolated monasteries in Europe tried it on one another in Latin.

The details of the riddle vary from place to place. Often a family must cross a river, or some missionaries and cannibals must do so. Or it is a farmer on his way home with some new animals.

Usually the boat they have is far too small to carry all of them at the same time. There also may be other dangers. But the problem is always the same: How can they safely reach the other shore?

1. No More Than a Hundred Pounds
A man, his wife, and their two young sons came to a

river they had to cross. On the riverbank they found a boat that they could use, but a notice inside the boat said that it could carry only one hundred pounds at a time.

The man weighed a hundred pounds and so did his wife. The boys each weighed about fifty pounds. How did they cross the river without overloading the boat?

2. A Fox, a Goose, and a Sack of Corn

A farmer went to market and bought a fox, a goose, and a sack of seed corn. On his way home, he had to cross a river. But the boat was so small, he could take only one of his new possessions across at a time. And that created a problem.

If he took the sack of corn across, he would be leaving the fox and the goose together, and the fox would eat the goose.

If he took the fox across, he would be leaving the goose and the corn alone, and the goose would eat the corn.

The only things he could leave together safely were the fox and the corn, for foxes don't like corn.

How did he manage to move all three safely to the other side of the river?

SOLUTIONS.

1. No More Than a Hundred Pounds
    A. The two boys got into the boat first and rowed across. One of the boys went ashore, and the other rowed back by himself.
    B. Their mother then rowed across by herself. The boy who already was there rowed back alone.
    C. The two boys again crossed the river. One stayed with his mother, and the other rowed back by himself.

D. Their father rowed across by himself. Then the boy who was there with his mother rowed back alone.

E. The two boys rowed across once again. But this time they pulled the boat out of the water, and the family continued on its way.

2. A Fox, a Goose, and a Sack of Corn

A. The farmer rowed the goose across and returned by himself.

B. He then moved the corn across. He rowed back with the goose so that it would not eat the corn.

C. He rowed the fox across, leaving it with the corn. He then returned by himself.

D. He took the goose across for the last time and headed for home.

If you guessed that the farmer moved the fox second and the corn third, that's all right, too—as long as you kept the goose away from both of them.

15

More Riddle Jokes

These are as silly as the riddle jokes in Chapter 2.

1. Why is it wrong to whisper?

2. What is the best way to catch a rabbit?

3. What is yellow and buzzes and grows on trees?

4. Why did the owl howl?

5. What should you know before you try to teach a dog tricks?

6. What do you get when you cross a canary with a tiger?

7. What is the difference between a zoo and a delica-
   tessen?

8. What is green and flies through the air faster
   than a speeding bullet?

9. Why can't a nose be twelve inches long?

10. What did the bald man say when he got a comb
    for his birthday?

SOLUTIONS

1. It isn't aloud.

2. Hide behind a bush and make a noise like a carrot.

3. An electric banana.

4. Because a woodpecker would peck 'er.

5. You should know more than the dog.

6. I don't know, but when it sings you'd better listen.

7. In a zoo there is a man-eating tiger. In a deli there is a man eating herring.

8. Super-Pickle.

9. Because then it would be a foot.

10. "I'll never part with this."

— 16 —

Tom and Bob

Two boys named Tom and Bob moved to town with their mother and father. The boys were twins. No one could tell them apart except their parents. They looked so much alike, they went to different schools. Otherwise they would have confused their teachers and classmates.

Toward the end of the term, Bob's teacher told him that he might win a prize for having the best marks in his grade.

"But first," said the teacher, "you'll have to solve three riddles. That is a tradition in our school. One of them is 'How deep is the ocean?' Another is 'How many stars are there in the sky?' The third one is 'What am I thinking?' I'll ask you for the answers tomorrow."

When Bob got home, he was very gloomy. Tom asked him what was bothering him. "Tomorrow the teacher is going to give me three riddles I have to solve before I can get the prize," said Bob. "And I don't think I can answer them." He told Tom what they were.

"Don't worry," said Tom. "I'll answer them for you. I'll go to your school and make believe I'm you. You go to my school and make believe you're me. Nobody will know the difference."

The next morning each boy went to the other's school, and Tom was right—nobody knew the difference. After Bob's teacher took attendance, he asked Bob (really Tom) to solve the three riddles.

"How deep is the ocean?" the teacher asked.

"A stone's throw," said the boy.

"What do you mean by that?" the teacher asked.

"When you throw a stone into the water," said the boy, "it always goes straight to the bottom."

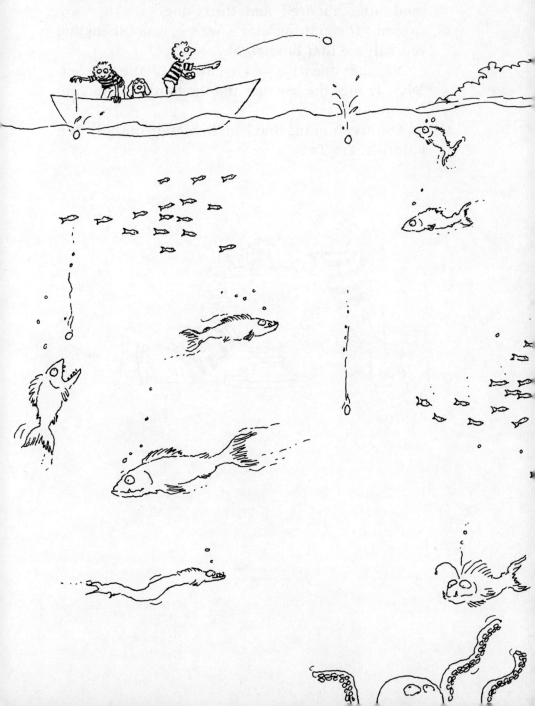

"Very good," said the teacher. "Here is the second one. How many stars are there in the sky?"

"There are four million two hundred and ten thousand nine hundred and thirty-one," the boy answered. "If you think that is wrong, count them and you will see that I am right."

"No, that seems about right," said the teacher. "Now here is the last one and the hardest. What am I thinking?"

"You are thinking that I am Bob," said the boy. "But I am not. I'm Tom."

— 17 —
Queer-Word Riddles

A man stood on his tipper tillies
Looking through his wipper willies.
Saw a phoebe chase a fobby
Through a bed of wibby wobby.

Riddles like this one from New York State are among
the strangest in the English language. Each has its
own set of queer words that somebody made up for
the fun of it. Often these words were based on how
something looked or sounded or seemed to the riddler.

In the riddle above, "tipper tillies" are tiptoes,
"wipper willies" are eyeglasses, a "phoebe" is a fox,
a "fobby" is a rabbit, and "wibby wobby" is a crop of
some kind.

These riddles may seem mysterious, but usually they are about one part of farm life or another. There aren't any queer-word riddles about city life or life in the suburbs. Perhaps someone who reads this will make some up.

1. As I went up my wimmey wommins,
    I peeked out my gimmey gommins,
    I saw belfoggins rooting up my fummey foggins.
    I called Peter Pelter, set him on belfoggins,
    For rooting up my fummey foggins.

    What is going on?

2. As I sat in my tintle-tontle,
    I saw a findle carry my fondle
        over the hingle-jingle.
    I hollered to my whirly-burly
        to fetch me my humble-bumble
    To stop the findle carrying my fondle
        over the hingle-jingle.

    What has happened now?

3. My mother sent me to your mother
    To borrow the whimble-bo, whamble-bo,
    The iron-body, the fore-body,
    The lil-lika-lal-lecka whirligig.

    What did the boy or girl borrow?

SOLUTIONS

1. "Whimmey wommins" is a staircase, "gimmey gommins" are eyeglasses, "belfoggins" is a hog, "fummey foggins" are potatoes, and "Peter Pelter" is a dog.

2. "Tintle-tontle" is a house, "findle" is a fox, "fondle" is a goose, "hingle-jingle" is a hill, "whirly-burly" is a wife, and "humble-bumble" is a shotgun.

3. The boy or girl borrowed a spinning wheel. The "whimble-bo, whamble-bo, the iron-body, the fore-body" are names used in the riddle for parts of the wheel. The "lil-lika-lal-lecka" are sounds the wheel made. A "whirligig" is something that whirls around and around.

— 18 —

The Great Castle
Strawbungle

There once was a farmer who wanted everyone to think that he was the most elegant person they had ever met. When he hired a new servant boy, he told him that everybody on the farm had a special name he was to use.

The farmer was to be called "Master of All Masters." The farmer's wife was the "Great Dame of Paradise." Their daughter was "Maid Stride-a-Bush," and their cat was "Gray-Faced Jeffer."

All sorts of things also had special names. The

farmhouse was "The Great Castle Strawbungle." The barn was "Mount Potago." The farmer's bed was the "Easy Decree." His trousers were "Struntifers." A fire was "Great Glory," and water was "Don Nippery Septo." There were many more such names, but for now these are all we need to know.

The servant boy learned all of them that night. The next morning he was up bright and early to cook breakfast for the family. When he made the fire, the farmer's cat snuggled down nearby and closed his eyes. "Good morning, Gray-Faced Jeffer," the boy said, and the cat purred.

Just then a spark flew out of the fireplace and landed on Jeffer's big, bushy tail. When his tail began to burn, the cat let out a terrible yowl and dashed out of the kitchen and into the barn.

In that season the barn was filled with dry hay. When Jeffer arrived, the hay caught fire, and the boy dashed upstairs to get the farmer.

"Master of All Masters!" he shouted. "Rise up from your Easy Decree! Pull on your Struntifers! Wake up the Great Dame of Paradise! Wake up Maid Stride-a-Bush! Gray-Faced Jeffer has brought Great Glory to Mount Potago! Without Don Nippery Septo, Mount Potago will soon be gone! So will the Great Castle Strawbungle—and all of us!"

To his credit, the boy got every one of those elegant names right. But when the farmer finally woke up, he could not remember what most of them meant. He was forever changing them, and now he was completely confused.

"What kind of a queer riddle is this?" he cried. "Tell it again!" While the servant boy told it again, and again, and tried to explain, Mount Potago burned to the ground. But Gray-Faced Jeffer escaped, and so did the rest of them.

19
Hidden Answers

The answers to these old riddles are hidden in the riddles themselves. The solution may be just one of the words in a riddle or even part of a word. Or it may be two or three words that must be run together to get the answer. Here is an example.

> As I was going down the lane,
> I met a man doing just the same.
> He tipped his hat and drew his cane,
> And in this riddle I have told you his name.

What is it?

For the answer, look in the third line of the riddle. The name is "Andrew," from the words "and" and "drew."

In some of these riddles the answer is a letter of the alphabet. Usually the riddle tells you where to find it.

It is in the church,
But not in the steeple.
It is in the parson,
But not in the people.

What is it?

As the riddle explains, the answer is in the "church," but not in the "steeple," in the "parson," but not in the "people." The only letter in both "church" and "parson" is the letter "r." Now try these.

1. Around the corner there is a tree.
    Under the tree there is a school.
    In the school there is a desk.
    On the desk there is a bell.
    Behind the desk there is a teacher.

    What is her name?

2. Lewis Carroll, the author of *Alice in Wonderland*, made up this hidden-answer riddle for some children he knew.

    Dreaming of apples on a wall,
    And dreaming often, dear,
    I dreamed that if I counted all—
    How many would appear?

    Of how many apples did Carroll dream?

3. There is a thing in Amsterdam,
   In Rome it too appears,
   You see it twice in every moment,
   But not once in seven years.

   What is it?

4. In the garden was a river,
   In the river, on a hot summer's eve, was a boat.
   In the boat was a lady with a bright red petticoat.
   If you don't know her name
   You only have yourself to blame.

5. It is between heaven and earth,
   And not in a tree.
   Now I've told you the answer
   As plain as can be.

   What is it?

   The next two riddles also have their answers hidden in them.

6. What is the difference between "here" and "there"?

7. What is the end of everything?

SOLUTIONS

1. The teacher's first name is Isabelle. It is found in the fourth line of the riddle, in the words "is a bell."

2. Lewis Carroll dreamed of ten apples. The answer is in the second line of the riddle, in the word "often," or "of ten."

3. It is the letter "m." It is found twice in "Amsterdam," once in "Rome," and twice in "moment," but not once in "seven years."

4. The lady's name is Eve. It is in the second line of the riddle.

5. It is a "knot" in a tree, which is mentioned in the second line. The word is spelled "not" in the riddle, but it will sound like "knot" to someone who hears it.

6. The difference between "here" and "there" is the letter "t."

7. The letter "g" is at the end of the word "everything."

20

More Tricky Questions

These are like the riddles in Chapter 4. Just find the trick, and you will find the answer.

1. A barrel weighed twenty pounds. But after a man put something in it, the barrel weighed only fifteen pounds. What did he put in it?

2. Two girls were playing checkers. They played five games, and each won the same number. How could that be? P.S. There were no ties.

3. When do two and two make more than four?

4. What can you hold in your left hand, but not in your right hand?

5. If it took five men one day to dig up a field, how long will it take ten men to dig up the same field?

6. One of the words on this page is mispelled. Which word is it?

7. A family built a big square house with each side facing south. A big bear wandered by. What color was the bear?

8. Where did John Hancock sign the Declaration of Independence?

9. What has a foot on each side and one in the middle?

10. If it takes a woodpecker eight months to peck a four-inch hole in a tree, how long would it take a grasshopper to kick all the seeds out of a pickle seven inches long and three inches thick?

SOLUTIONS

1. A big hole.

2. They played different opponents.

3. When they are used to make twenty-two.

4. Your right elbow.

5. No time at all. The field has already been dug up.

6. The word "mispelled" is the word that is mis-spelled.

7. The house was built at the North Pole. That is the only place on Earth where each side would face south. The only bears in that region are polar bears. So the bear that wandered by was white.

8. At the bottom.

9. A yardstick.

10. If your friends say, "There isn't any answer!" they are right!

— 21 —
"If You Can Unriddle That, You Can Hang Me."

A man is about to be hanged for a crime. But before the sentence is carried out, he is given one last chance to escape death. If he can ask a riddle that the judge cannot solve, he will save his neck and go free.

There are several riddle tales like this, each with a neck-saving riddle of its own. The strangest thing about these "neck riddles" is that there is no way for the judge in the story to unriddle them. Each concerns something that only the prisoner knows about.

Here is a neck riddle from Texas:

Horn ate horn in a high oak tree.

And here is the solution. A fellow named Horn was accused of stealing cattle. When the sheriff's deputies came after him, he took to the woods. They hunted high and low for Horn, but they could not find him.

He had climbed up into a big oak tree. There he hid in a tangle of vines, like a fat possum, waiting for them to give up and search elsewhere. But when one of the deputies looked up and saw him, Horn knew that there was no chance to escape. He slid down one of the vines and gave up.

When they got him to town, the judge, who also was the barber, heard the case right then and there. He found Horn guilty and sentenced him to hang. But

then he smiled and said, "I'll turn you loose if you can ask me a riddle I can't solve."

Horn was so scared of being hanged, he couldn't think of a thing. He just stood there fidgeting, didn't say a word. But as they were about to take him out and string him up, a riddle came to him.

"I've thought of one," he said in a small voice. "Here it is: Horn ate horn in a high oak tree.

"If you can unriddle that, you can hang me."

The judge and the others knew the riddle was about Horn, but they could not figure out what it meant. They guessed and guessed, but they got nowhere. Finally they gave up, and Horn explained it to them.

"While you were hunting for me," he said, "I lived high in that oak tree the whole time. I didn't come down once, and after a while I got awful hungry. Well, I had an old cow horn that I carried with me. If I was in trouble, I'd blow into it to get help. I gnawed at that horn just like a dog gnaws at a bone, hoping to find something to eat. That's what my riddle means."

He pulled a piece of the horn from his pocket. It had tooth marks on it. He showed it to the judge as proof, and the judge set him free.

Here is a neck riddle that was told in many places:

As I went out and in again,
From the dead the living came.
Six there were, and seven there will be.

79

And here is the solution. During a long drought a man was found guilty of stealing water for his livestock. It was a very serious crime, and he was sentenced to hang.

But it was the first time he had been in trouble. So the judge told the prisoner that he would set him free if he asked a riddle the judge could not solve. He gave him three days to go off and think of one.

As the man left the jail, he noticed the skull of a steer at the side of the road. Then he put it out of his mind. He had more important things to think about. But after three days he still did not have a riddle that would save him. He rode back toward town filled with dread.

As he headed for the jail, the skull of the steer again caught his eye. But now there was a bird's nest in the skull. Inside he saw six young birds and the egg of a seventh. He thought about it for a while, then made up a riddle about what he had seen.

When the judge asked if he had a riddle to try, he gave this one:

> "As I went out and in again,
> From the dead the living came.
> Six there were, and seven there will be."

Then he added:

"Answer this riddle or set me free."

The judge could not make anything of the riddle. Neither could anyone else at the jail. So the prisoner told them about seeing the skull of a dead steer and the bird's nest inside with six young birds and the egg of a seventh.

The judge sent the sheriff out to check the skull. When he came back, he said it was just the way the prisoner had described it. So the judge set him free.

There may have been a time when riddles actually were used by prisoners to win their freedom. Some say it was a custom in parts of the South and the Southwest in the United States before there was a system of judges and juries.

There also are stories about blacks in the South who won their freedom from jail in a similar way. But instead of riddling, they sang their way out. They made up songs in which they explained their crimes and pleaded for freedom. Then they tried to sing them for the judges or the wardens of their jails or anyone else who could help.

It is said that Huddie Ledbetter, who became the famous blues singer Leadbelly, sang his way out of the Texas Central Prison Farm in the 1920s or 1930s. Another blues singer, "Lightnin'" Sam Hopkins, may have gotten his freedom from a prison in East Texas in the same way.

22

Leg Riddles

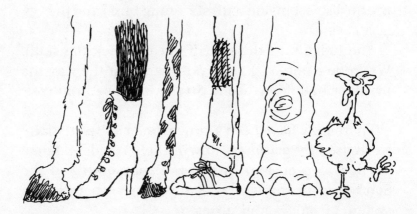

In these riddles each set of legs stands for a person, an animal, or something else. When you figure out what the legs describe, you have solved the riddle.

A leg riddle was included in one of the first riddle books published in the English language. It was the *Book of Meery [Merry] Riddles*, which appeared in England in 1629. Here is part of that riddle:

"Two legs sat upon three legs and had one leg in her hand. Then in came four legs and carried away one leg. . . ."

What does it mean? A person (two legs) sat on a stool (three legs) and had a leg of mutton (one leg) in his or her hand. Then in came a dog (four legs) and carried away the leg of mutton. . . .

Now try these:

1. Two legs sat upon three legs filling a pail while four legs waited patiently. Then four legs, with one leg, kicked two legs off three legs. Then two legs hit four legs with three legs.

2. Four legs sat on four legs waiting for four legs to come out of its hole.

3. Two legs sat upon four legs eating one leg. In came four legs—and out went four legs with one leg! Close behind was two legs, without one leg, shaking four legs at four legs.

SOLUTIONS

1. A girl (or a boy) sat upon a stool milking a cow. Then the cow, using one of its legs, kicked the girl off the stool. Then the girl hit the cow with the stool.

2. A cat sat on a table waiting for a mouse (or a rat) to come out of its hole.

3. A girl (or a boy) sat on a chair eating a chicken leg. In came the dog—and out it went with the chicken leg! Close behind was the girl, without the chicken leg, shaking the chair at the dog.

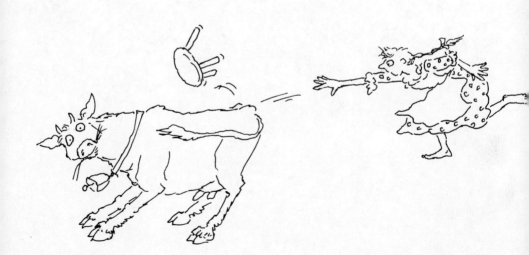

23
True Riddles

The true riddle is the oldest kind of riddle we have.
It was invented thousands of years ago by some un-
known person who must have loved word riddles.

Most true riddles are about ordinary things, like an
egg, a tooth, a thimble, or the wind. But they describe
such things in the most surprising ways.

In one riddle the wind is seen as a noisy old man
named Boris.*

> Old Father Boris came to the door,
> He came with a dash and a rush and a roar.
> He whooped and he hollered,
>   and he made a great din,
> And at last the old fellow
>   popped right in.

---

*"Boris" once was "Boreas," the name ancient Greeks gave to the
north wind.

In another riddle, a thimble is thought of as a strange and terrible barrel.

A bottomless barrel,
It is shaped like a hive.
It is filled with flesh.
And the flesh is *alive!*

In still another, an egg is described as a strange store, a kind of butcher shop.

In the meadow there is a white store.
It is filled with meat, but there is no door.

To solve a true riddle, you must figure out what the riddle is really describing. In the riddles above, it is not a noisy old man. It is the wind. It is not a barrel of flesh, but a thimble that looks like a tiny barrel. And it is not a store. It is an egg.

A number of true riddles have two parts, which makes them easier to solve. In the first part, the riddle tries to trick you by suggesting the wrong answer. But in the second part, it changes what it said earlier and points to the right answer. This old riddle about Nancy Etticoat is an example:

Little Nancy Etticoat
In a white petticoat
    and a red nose,
The longer she stands,
    the shorter she grows.

First you learn that this riddle is about a girl who has a white petticoat and a red nose. But then you are told that the longer she stands, the shorter she grows.

Since living creatures do not grow shorter and shorter, the riddle must be describing something else that behaves this way, something that is not alive.

What is red at the top, white all over, and grows shorter the longer it stands? A candle burning!

There is one thing to remember about true riddles. All the clues you need usually are right there in the riddle. Once you get enough practice, you will be able to solve quite a few.

1. First you see me in the grass
   Dressed in yellow gay.
   Then I dress all in white,
   Then I fly away.

2. Out in the field there is a green house.
   Inside the green house, there is a white house.
   Inside the white house, there is a red house.
   Inside the red house,
       there are a lot of little babies,
       black and white.

3. You throw away the outside
       and cook the inside.
   Then you eat the outside
       and throw away the inside.

4. What goes up white and comes down yellow?

5. Something is broken. Then it is used.

6. Humpy Bumpy on the wall,
Humpy Bumpy got a fall.
Ten men, a thousand more,
Can't fix Humpy Bumpy back
   like it was before.

7. Though I dance at a ball,
I am nothing at all.

8. What has feet and legs, and nothing else?

9. Tie them up and they walk.
Untie them and they sleep.

10. I run uphill and downhill,
But I never move an inch.

11. A red dancer dances in a red room,
   with white chairs set all around.

12. Behind a thick hedge of bones,
A small dog barks, then moans.

13. Thirty white horses on a red hill,
Now they dance, now they prance,
Now they stand still.

14. What is it that belongs to you,
yet is used by others more than by you?

15. Red and blue, purple and green.
No one can reach it,
Not even a queen.

SOLUTIONS

1. A dandelion.

2. A watermelon.

3. An ear of corn.

4. An egg.

5. An egg.

6. An egg.

7. A shadow.

8. A pair of stockings.

9. A pair of shoes.

10. A path or a road.

11. The tongue, mouth, and teeth.

12. The teeth and the tongue.

13. The teeth and the gums.

14. Your name.

15. A rainbow.

Notes,
Sources,
and
Bibliography

Abbreviations in Notes, Sources, and Bibliography

BL	Boys' Life, "Think and Grin" columns
CFQ	California Folklore Quarterly
JAF	Journal of American Folklore
KFQ	Keystone Folklore Quarterly
KFR	Kentucky Folklore Record
MAFS	Memoirs of the American Folklore Society
MF	Midwest Folklore
MFA	Maryland Folklore Archive, University of Maryland, College Park
NCFJ	North Carolina Folklore Journal
NYFA	Folklore Archive, New York State Historical Association, Cooperstown
NYFQ	New York Folklore Quarterly
RU	Compiler's collection of folklore, contributed by his students at Rutgers University, New Brunswick, N.J., 1963–78.
SFQ	Southern Folklore Quarterly
UPFA	University of Pennsylvania Folklore Archive, Philadelphia
WF	Western Folklore

Notes

The publications cited are described in the bibliography.

Magic, Riddle Wars, and the Sphinx. Several thousand years ago riddles played an important part in everyday life. People believed there was magic in riddles. If they answered certain ones correctly, the gods would see to it that their crops would grow, or that a boy would grow to be a man, or that the spirit of a dead person would not haunt them.

Over the centuries, riddles became part of the traditions and ceremonies in many religions. One finds riddles in the Old Testament and the New Testament, in the Koran of Islam, and in the Rig-Veda, the most holy book of Hindu hymns. One of these hymns contains fifty-one riddles.

In some places women used riddles to help choose husbands. In parts of Turkey a suitor who could not solve three riddles in succession was thought to be stupid and was sent on his way. When a wedding took place, riddling and unriddling were part of the ceremony. If the bride and groom could answer the riddles asked of them, it was a sign that all would go well in their marriage.

For hundreds of years there also were riddling matches in many countries. In ancient Greece and Rome, these contests took place at banquets and other celebrations. A riddle master selected a riddle, which was passed from person to person until someone solved it. That person was given a wreath of laurel leaves to wear on his or her head. But those who failed to solve the riddle had to drink a glass of salt water mixed with wine.

Some riddling matches, or "riddle wars," as they were called, involved kings, queens, and other important people. They competed to decide who was the most skillful riddler. Solomon, king of the ancient Hebrews, and the Queen of Sheba had such a match. So did the kings of Babylonia, Tyre, Egypt, Ethiopia, and other nations.

Some even hired experts to help them decide which riddles to ask and which solutions to give. One of these experts was Aesop, the famous Greek writer of fables. Another was Abdemon, a famous magician who helped King Hiram of Tyre to defeat King Solomon for the first time.

Often great riches were wagered on the outcome of these riddle wars. When Solomon won his match with the Queen of Sheba, he won a large store of gold, jewels, and spices. In riddle wars among tribal chieftains in Hawaii, the stakes were even higher. At times a loser was boiled in water.

The most famous riddling match of all probably was the contest between a young Greek named Oedipus and the Sphinx, a creature with the head of a woman, the body of a lion, and the wings of an eagle.

As the story is told, the Sphinx had been sent to the city of Thebes to punish the people for the crimes of their king.

She waited on a rock that overlooked the city and she asked this question of everyone who passed:

"What walks on four legs in the morning, on two legs at noon, and on three in the evening?"

No one could solve it, and everyone who failed died at her hand. Then Oedipus solved it and brought an end to her reign of terror.

The answer he gave was "man." In the "morning" of his life, when he is quite young, man creeps on all fours. At the high point of his life, at "noon," he walks erect on two legs. In the "evening" of his life, when he grows old and feeble, he walks with the help of a cane, or on three legs.

When Oedipus gave his answer, the Sphinx leaped from the rock to her death.

See Potter; Kelso; Solomon, pp. 86–88; Köngäs-Miranda, p. 127.

Where Riddles Come From. Most of the riddles we know are folk riddles. They were created by ordinary people whose names have been forgotten. But their riddles have passed from person to person and from place to place. Some have been on the move for hundreds, even thousands, of years.

The rest of our riddles have come from novelists, poets, and other writers. They are called "literary riddles." Some actually are folk riddles that writers have retold. Others are original riddles they have created.

In the seventeenth and eighteenth centuries there were a great many writers who composed riddles. They included Jonathan Swift, Jean Jacques Rousseau, Johann von Goethe, and François Voltaire. The sixth riddle in Chapter 9 is a shortened version of a riddle by Voltaire.

In the nineteenth century one of the best known of the literary riddlers was Lewis Carroll, who made up riddles for the young people he knew. See Chapter 19, #2. But in the twentieth century this practice seems to have died.

See Taylor, *CFQ* 2, pp. 143–45, and *SFQ* 11; Fisher, pp. 61–67.

Riddle Jokes (Chapters 2, 15). "Riddle jokes" are so named because of the question-and-answer format they use. They tend to deal with subjects that briefly have caught the public's fancy, such as pickles or elephants or imaginary animals.

The prototypes for these jokes often are created by professional jokesmiths whose work appears in paperback books or on radio or TV. If their jokes catch on, they provide models for jokes that members of the public may coin. And if *their* jokes take hold, a cycle of riddle jokes develops.

These riddles usually are of two types. A number are conundrums, a form that goes back at least to the seventeenth century. They make use of a pun or some other word play and an unexpected answer. "How does a witch tell time?" is a modern conundrum based on a pun. The answer: "With a witch watch."

Other riddle jokes are classified as "riddling questions." They too rely on the unexpected answer, but they do not use word play. "What is the best way to catch a rabbit?" in Chapter 15 is an example. The answer: "Hide behind a bush and make a noise like a carrot." See Taylor, *CFQ* 2, pp. 145–47.

The Giraffe's Neck (Chapter 2, #9). The riddle about the giraffe's neck resembles a question Abraham Lincoln once was asked. "How long should a man's legs be when they are in proportion to his body?" an acquaintance wanted to know. "Only long enough to reach the ground," Lincoln is said to have replied.

Humdingers (Chapter 2, #10). The "humdinger" is one of many imaginary animals that appeared in the 1960s as part of a cycle of riddle jokes. Each of these imaginary animals resulted from combining the traits of two living creatures or of one living creature and an inanimate object. In the case of the humdinger, it was a bee and a bell.

This type of riddle is related to one that was popular in England several hundred years ago. Here also the characteristics of two creatures were combined. One of these riddles asks, "What has eight legs, two arms, and wings?" The answer: "A man on horseback carrying a canary." See Abrahams and Hickerson; Taylor, *WF* 22.

Droodles (Chapter 5). Creating droodles and solving them became a national pastime in the United States in the 1950s. This was a result of a series of best-selling books of droodles by Roger Price, as well as a national TV quiz show about them. In that period you also could buy a tie or a napkin with droodles on it, or a piece of jewelry in the shape of a droodle. See Bowman.

I'm My Own Grandpaw (Chapter 7). How could this be? A popular song of the 1940s, "I'm My Own Grandpaw," explained it this way:

1. A young man married an older woman who had a grown daughter.

2. As a result, her daughter then became his stepdaughter.

3. The young man's father, who no longer had a wife, fell in love with his son's stepdaughter and married her.

4. When that happened, the young man's stepdaughter also became his stepmother. He then was not only her stepfather, but her stepson.

5. When that happened, the mother of his new stepmother became his step-grandmother. (Of course, she already was his wife.)

6. And when that happened, he became her step-grandchild. Since he already was married to his step-grandmother, he also became his own grandpaw!

Things became even more confused when the young man and his wife had a baby, and the young man's father and stepmother/stepdaughter also had one.

For similar riddles circulated during the nineteenth century, see Bombaugh, p. 186.

Rebus Riddles (Chapter 11). During the late nineteenth century, rebus riddles like those in Chapter 11 were used in picture-puzzle contests run by major newspapers in England and America. The idea was to attract new readers. See Dudeney, p. 55.

King John and the Bishop (Chapter 16). This is the international tale on which the story "Tom and Bob" is based. The tale is known in America and England through the ballad "King John and the Bishop." Its title elsewhere is "The Emperor and the Abbot."

King John has been angered by the luxurious way in which the bishop lives. He summons him to the palace and gives him three riddles to answer within a certain period of time. The riddles are similar to those in "Tom an Bob." If he does not answer all of them correctly, the king will order his execution.

The bishop's miller or shepherd volunteers to dress as the bishop and answer the questions in his place. He answers them correctly and saves the bishop's life.

The story is of great interest to folklore scholars because of the extensive research the folklorist Walter Anderson carried out into its development and distribution. There are some six hundred variants of the story, including "Tom and Bob." See Thompson, pp. 161–62.

Queer-Word Riddles (Chapters 17, 18). Some scholars link the use of queer-word riddles in modern times to an ancient custom some primitive tribes practiced.

Members of these tribes believed that they could be harmed through magic if some evil person misused their given names. As a result, blood relatives were not permitted to disclose these names or use words that resembled them. In some tribes a word that had even a single syllable in common with a given name was taboo. Nonsense words were used in their place.

The custom was practiced by some North American Indian and Eskimo tribes, by tribes in Central and South America, by ancient Egyptians, Australian aborigines, and others. See Frazer, pp. 244–51; Long.

The Samson Riddle (Chapter 21). The neck riddle of the steer's skull or the horse's skull is based on a riddle that the Hebrew warrior Samson is said to have created three thousand years ago.

According to the legend, Samson was traveling on foot through the desert when he was attacked by a young lion. Never had Samson felt so strong, and he stood his ground and fought back. With his bare hands, he tore the lion limb from limb.

Several weeks later he passed that way again and came upon the lion's carcass, just as the prisoner came upon the skull of the steer. Only now the carcass was filled with a honeycomb a swarm of bees had left, just as the skull was filled with young birds. Samson made up a riddle about this experience, just as the prisoner did thousands of years later. This was Samson's riddle:

> Out of the eater came something to eat,
> and out of the strong came something sweet.

Of course, no one could solve the riddle unless they knew about his experiences with the lion, which also was true of the prisoner's riddle and the prisoner's experiences. The Samson riddle is in the Book of Judges 14:14 of the Old Testament. See Potter, pp. 941–42; Abrahams, p. 8.

Sources

The source of each item is given, along with variants and related information. Where available, the names of collectors (C) and informants (I) are given. Publications cited are described in the Bibliography.

1. NO WAY OUT
This riddle is retold from four well-known variants, each with a different solution.

2. RIDDLE JOKES
1. UPFA, I: Melodi Barrick, 4, Carlisle, Pa., 1965. C: Mac E. Barrick.
2. RU, 1972.
3. I: Kenneth Goldstein, Philadelphia, 1980.
4. RU, 1978.
5. I: Marsha Valance, Dubuque, Ia., 1980. Abridged slightly.
6. RU, 1972.

7. RU, 1970.
8. Solomon and Solomon, p. 93, from Alabama.
9. MFA, 1970.
10. Abrahams and Hickerson, p. 255.

3. STRANGE HAPPENINGS

1. Moore, p. 121. #9, from North Carolina. Retold.
2. Moore, p. 122, #16, from North Carolina. Retold.
3. Retold from variants in Kinnaird, p. 224; "The Race to Mecca"; Moore, p. 122, #15.
4. I: Eric Mann, 10, Mesa, Ariz., 1982; Erin Hooker, 12, Parkway School, Mt. Laurel Township, N.J., 1982. Retold.
5. Retold from Kinnaird, p. 414.
6. I: Bryan Hunt, 12, Mt. Laurel Township, N.J., 1982. Also see Moore, p. 122, #14; Browne and Brooks, p. 160. Retold.

4. TRICKY QUESTIONS

1. RU, 1972.
2. Puzzlewit, p. 19.
3. Ainsworth, p. 294, #520, from Pontiac, Mich.
4. McDowell, p. 253, #74, from Texas.
5. Johnson, p. 151, from New England.
6. UPFA, 1972.
7. Brewster, p. 100, #3, from southern Indiana.
8. Clark, p. 119, #78, from North Carolina.
9. Traditional catch.
10. Randolph and Spradley, p. 89.
11. Traditional catch. This first was recorded in the English language in *Demaundes Joyous*, a riddle book published in England in 1511 from a French collection, as quoted in Opie, 1959, p. 73.
12. Traditional problem riddle. Peter DeVries included a version in his novel *The Tunnel of Love*, p. 32.

5. DROODLES

Chapter introduction: giraffe droodle, I: Sean Hanifin, Swarthmore College, Swarthmore, Pa., 1978; beggar's cup droodle, Posner, p. 65.

1. I: Sean Hanifin.
2. RU, 1972. See Roemer, p. 182.
3. Bowman, p. 25.
4. I: Sean Hanifin.
5. RU, 1972.
6. I: Sean Hanifin.
7. I: Lisa Greenfield, 12, Natick, Mass., 1979. C: Cindy Lewis, Framingham State College, Framingham, Mass.
8. RU, 1972.
9. RU, 1972.
10. RU, 1974. See Roemer, p. 175.

The giraffe droodle and droodles 1 to 6 and 8 to 10 derive from various books and newspaper articles by Price in the 1950s and 1960s.

6. WHAT DOES G H O T I *REALLY* SPELL?

Compiler's childhood recollection, Brooklyn, N.Y., 1940s. As James Joyce explained in *Finnegan's Wake*, "Gee each [aitch] owe tea eye smells fish. That's U."

7. I'M MY OWN GRANDPAW

Chapter heading is taken from the title of a song, "I'm My Own Grandpaw," by Dwight Latham and Moe Jaffe, the General Music Publishing Co., 1947.

1. Compiler's recollection.
2. Evans, p. 175, from Mississippi.
3. Taylor, *JAF* 51, p. 33.
4. RU, 1972.
5. Loyd, 1914, p. 336.
6. RU, 1972.

7. Taylor, *JAF* 51, p. 33.
8. Ainsworth, p. 291, #475, from Fairfield, Ill.

8. ELEPHANT RIDDLES

1. Barrick, *SFQ*, p. 272, #36, from Pennsylvania.
2. Barrick, *KFQ*, p. 70, #88, from Pennsylvania prior to 1946.
3. *BL*, 7–63.
4. *BL*, 12–63; "Elephants by the Trunk."
5. *BL*, 12–63.
6. Barrick, *SFQ* p. 276, #77, from Pennsylvania.

9. WHO AM I? WHAT AM I?

1. Adams, #32.
2. *Puzzledom*, #32.
3. Adams, #31.
4. Adams, #126.
5. Ward, p. 62.
6. Dudeney, p. 7.

All the selections in this chapter are adapted.

10. A PUNCTUATION RIDDLE

Traditional punctuation riddle. Adapted. For a complete version, see Dudeney, pp. 98–99. For two similar riddles, see Schwartz, pp. 84–85.

11. REBUS RIDDLES

All entries are from Loyd, 1912: the radish rebus in the chapter introduction, p. 104; 1, p. 4; 2, p. 69; 3, p. 100; 4, p. 32; 5, p. 75; 6, p. 19; 7, p. 112; 8, p. 114; 9, p. 119; 10, p. 72.

12. WHAT NEVER WAS AND NEVER WILL BE?

Ainsworth, p. 277, #25. When this entry appeared in the English riddle book *Demaundes Joyous* over four hundred years ago, it asked, "What thing is that which never was nor never will be?" Its modern version has just been shortened a bit.

13. LETTER RIDDLES

1. Dudeney, p. 9, #13. Adapted.
2. *Aunt Sue's Budget*, p. 59.
3. RU, 1977.
4. Espy, p. 209.

14. CROSSING THE RIVER

1, 2. Traditional riddle. For some variants, see Johnson,
p. 149, 150; Ainsworth, p. 292, #493; Smith and Dale,
p. 333; Hull, p. 281, #301; Fauset, *JAF* 40, p. 291.

15. MORE RIDDLE JOKES

1. Ainsworth, p. 288, #415, from Pontiac, Mich.
2. Barrick, *SFQ*, p. 287, #208.
3. Compiler's recollection, 1970s.
4. RU, 1977.
5. Withers and Benet, p. 69.
6. I: Vicki Stout, 9, Green Street School, Phillipsburg, N.J.,
1978.
7. RU, 1977.
8. I: Mike Sullivan, 8, Tempe, Ariz., 1982.
9. RU, 1977.
10. *BL*, 6–53.

16. TOM AND BOB

A very brief version of this tale was collected from
Edwin Knowlton, Stonington, Me., 1975. The telling in this
book is based on that version and on a more detailed English variant in Jackson and Wilson, pp. 182–83. See *King
John and the Bishop* in the Notes.

17. QUEER-WORD RIDDLES

Chapter introduction: *NYFQ* 10, p. 108.
1. Redfield, *SFQ* 1, p. 44.
2. Randolph and Spradley, p. 87. Adapted.
3. Brewster, *SFQ* 3, p. 100.

18. THE GREAT CASTLE STRAWBUNGLE

This tale is retold from a number of variants. See Jackson and Wilson; Abrahams, pp. 110–12.

19. HIDDEN ANSWERS

Chapter introduction: "As I was going" and "It is in the church," I: Edwin Knowlton, Stonington, Me., 1975.

1. Ainsworth, p. 279, #268, from Fairfield, Ill.
2. Lewis Carroll, "Puzzles from Wonderland," in *Aunt Judy's Magazine*, Dec. 1890, as quoted in Fisher, pp. 64–65.
3. *Puzzledom*, p. 112, #97.
4. MFA, 1972.
5. I: Edwin Knowlton, Stonington, Me., 1975.
6. Solomon and Solomon, p. 93, from Alabama.
7. Ainsworth, p. 278, #257, from Fairfield, Ill.

20. MORE TRICKY QUESTIONS

1. Redfield, p. 42, #80, from middle Tennessee.
2. Camp Med-O-Lark *Almanac*, Washington, Me., Feb. 1975.
3. Camp Med-O-Lark *Almanac*.
4. Perkins, p. 113, #77, from New Orleans.
5. Compiler's recollection.
6. Camp Med-O-Lark *Almanac*.
7. Camp Med-O-Lark *Almanac*.
8. Compiler's recollection.
9. Compiler's recollection.
10. Randolph and Spradley, p. 87, from the Ozark Mountains region of Missouri and Arkansas. Adapted.

21. "IF YOU CAN UNRIDDLE THAT, YOU CAN HANG ME."

The riddle tale about Horn is retold from Randolph, 1955, pp. 36–37, and Braddy. The reference to the riddle of the bird's nest in a skull is from Solomon and Solomon,

p. 8, and Halpert, pp. 197–98, among many sources. For a discussion of the neck riddle form and its use in real life, see Abrahams, pp. 10–13, Norton, and Braddy. See *The Samson Riddle* in the Notes.

22. LEG RIDDLES

Chapter introduction: As quoted in Bombaugh, pp. 189–190.

1. Adapted from Halliwell-Phillips, p. 148, and Chappell, p. 229, #4.
2. Abrahams, p. 87, S-15, from Jamaica. Adapted.
3. Abrahams, p. 85, S-5, from Texas. Adapted.

23. TRUE RIDDLES

Chapter introduction: "Old Father Boris," Hudson, p. 90, #46; a "bottomless barrel," an Irish riddle that traveled to America, I: John Bishop, San Francisco, 1976; a "white store," Gardener, p. 256, from New York State; "Little Nancy Etticoat," traditional.

1. Emrich, 1955, p. 117. Adapted slightly.
2. Withers and Benet, p. 38. Widespread distribution in southeastern United States, with various endings. See Randolph and Spradley, p. 86; Fauset, *JAF* 40, p. 276, #3.
3. Ainsworth, p. 278, #253, from Pontiac, Mich.
4. Bacon and Parsons, p. 312, #2.
5. Taylor, 1951, #1137.
6. Taylor, 1951, #739. See Roberts, 1959, p. 140, from Kentucky.
7. This old riddle appears in a riddle book published in New Hampshire in 1807: Puzzlewit, p. 19.
8. Farr, p. 319, #21.
9. Emrich, 1955, p. 117. Adapted.
10. Emrich, 1955, p. 117.
11. Randolph and Parler, p. 257, from Arkansas.

12. RU, 1976.
13. Many sources. In one variant, the riddle concludes: "Now they champ, now they stamp/Now they stand still." See Potter, p. 939. Most texts describe thirty horses, or teeth, even though there are thirty-two. A few tell of twenty "horses," and there is one that describes sixty of them! See Fauset, *JAF* 40, #8.
14. Compiler's recollection.
15. Compiler's recollection. A similar version is reported from Arkansas: "What is red and blue/And purple and green/The king can't reach it/Neither can the queen." See Randolph and Parler, p. 257.

Bibliography

Books

Abrahams, Roger D. *The Living from the Dead: Riddles Which Tell Stories.* Helsinki: Folklore Fellows Communications, #225, 1980.

Adams, Samuel Hopkins, ed. *A Book of Clues for the Clever.* New York: Boni & Liveright, 1927.

Anderson, Walter. *Kaiser und Abt (The Emperor and the Abbot.)* Helsinki: Folklore Fellows Communications, #42, 1923.

Aunt Sue's Budget of Puzzles. New York: T. W. Strong, 1859.

Beckwith, Martha. *Hawaiian Mythology.* New Haven, Conn.: Yale University Press, 1940.

Bombaugh, C. C. *Gleanings for the Curious from the Harvest Fields of Literature*, 3rd ed. Philadelphia: J.B. Lippincott Co., 1890. Reprint edition: *Oddities and*

Curiosities of Words and Literature. New York: Dover Publications, Inc., 1961.

Brunvand, Jan A. *The Study of American Folklore*, 2nd ed. New York: W. W. Norton & Company, Inc., 1978.

Child, F. J., ed. *The English and Scottish Popular Ballads*, v. 1–6. Boston: Houghton Mifflin Company, 1894.

DeVries, Peter. *The Tunnel of Love.* Boston: Little, Brown and Company, 1954.

Dudeney, Henry E. *300 Best Word Puzzles.* New York: Charles Scribner's Sons, 1968.

Emrich, Duncan. *Folklore on the American Land.* Boston: Little, Brown and Company, 1972.

Esar, Evan. *The Humor of Humor.* New York: Horizon Press, 1952.

Espy, Willard. *The Game of Words.* New York: Grosset & Dunlap, Inc., 1971.

Fisher, John, ed. *The Magic of Lewis Carroll.* New York: Simon & Schuster, Inc., 1973.

Frazer, James G. *The Golden Bough: A Study in Magic and Religion*, abridged ed. New York: The Macmillan Company, 1940.

Gardener, Emelyn E. *Folklore from the Schoharie Hills.* Ann Arbor, Mich.: University of Michigan Press, 1937.

Halliwell-Phillips, James O. *The Nursery Rhymes of England.* London: Warne & Company, 1842.

Johnson, Clifton. *What They Say in New England and Other American Folklore.* Boston: Lee and Shepard, 1896. Reprint edition: Carl A. Withers, ed. New York: Columbia University Press, 1963.

Kinnaird, Clark. *Encyclopedia of Puzzles and Pastimes.* New York: Citadel Press, Inc., 1946.

Loyd, Sam. *Cyclopedia of Puzzles.* New York: Franklin Bigelow Corp., The Morningside Press, 1914.

———. *Sam Loyd's Puzzles (A Book for Children).* Philadelphia: David McKay Co., Inc., 1912.

McCosh, Sandra. *Children's Humour.* London: Granada Publishing, 1979.

McDowell, John H. *Children's Riddling.* Bloomington, Ind.: Indiana University Press, 1979.

Opie, Peter, and Iona Opie. *A Family Book of Nursery Rhymes.* New York: Oxford University Press, 1964.

————. *The Lore and Language of Schoolchildren.* New York: Oxford University Press, 1959.

————. *The Oxford Dictionary of Nursery Rhymes.* Oxford, England: Clarendon Press, 1951.

Posner, Donald. *Annibale Carracci*, v. 1. London: The Phaidon Press, Ltd., 1971. Includes samples of seventeenth-century "droodles."

Price, Roger. *The Compleat Droodle.* Los Angeles: Price, Stern, Sloan, 1962.

————. *Droodles.* New York: Simon & Schuster, Inc., 1953.

————. *Oodles of Droodles.* New York: Simon & Schuster, Inc., 1955.

————. *The Rich Sardine and Other New Droodles.* New York: Simon & Schuster, Inc., 1954.

Puzzledom, An Original Collection of Characters, Conundrums, etc. Philadelphia: William P. Hazard, 1854.

Puzzlewit, Peter (pseud.). *A Bag of Nuts Ready Crack'd, being a Choice Collection of Riddles, Paradoxes, etc.* Dover, N.H.: J. Whitlock, printer, 1807.

Randolph, Vance. *The Devil's Pretty Daughter and Other Ozark Tales.* New York: Columbia University Press, 1955.

————. *The Talking Turtle and Other Ozark Tales.* New York: Columbia University Press, 1957.

Roberts, Leonard. *Up Cutshin and Down Greasy.* Lexington, Ky.: University Press of Kentucky, 1959.

Schwartz, Alvin. *Flapdoodle: Pure Nonsense from American Folklore.* New York: J.B. Lippincott, 1980.

Shipley, Joseph T. *Word Games for Play and Power.* Englewood Cliffs, N.J.: Prentice-Hall, Inc., 1962.

Smith, Edwin W., and A. M. Dale. *The Ila-Speaking Peoples of Northern Rhodesia*, v. 2. London: Macmillan, and Co., Ltd., 1920.

Solomon, Jack, and Olivia Solomon. *Zickery Zan: Childhood Folklore.* University, Ala.: University of Alabama Press, 1980.

Taylor, Archer. *English Riddles from the Oral Tradition.* Berkeley, Cal.: University of California Press, 1951.

Thompson, Stith. *The Folktale.* New York: Holt, Rinehart, and Winston, Inc., 1946. Reprint edition: Berkeley, Cal.: University of California Press, 1977.

Ward, Susan H., and Mary L. Watson. *Green Guess Book.* New York: Dodd, Mead & Company, Inc., 1897.

Withers, Carl A., and Sula Benet. *The American Riddle Book.* New York: Abelard-Schuman Ltd., 1954.

Wiseman, Billy (pseud.). *Puzzle Cap: A Choice Collection of Riddles in Familiar Verse.* New York: John Low, 1800.

Wood, Ray. *Fun in American Folk Rhymes.* Philadelphia: J.B. Lippincott Co., 1952.

Articles

Abrahams, Roger D., and Joseph C. Hickerson. "Cross-Fertilization Riddles." *WF* 23 (1964): 253–57.

Ainsworth, Catherine H. "Black and White and Said All Over." *SFQ* 26 (1962): 263–95. Riddles from ninth- and tenth-grade classes in Arizona, Alaska, Connecticut, Illinois, Kentucky, Michigan, North Carolina.

Bacon, A. M., and E. C. Parsons. "Folklore from Elizabeth City County, Virginia." *JAF* 35 (1922): 250–327.

Barrick, Mac E. "The Newspaper Joke Riddle." *JAF* 87 (1974): 253–57.

———. "Riddles from Cumberland County." *KFQ* 8 (1963): 59–74.

———. "The Shaggy Elephant Riddle." *SFQ* 28 (1964): 266–90.

Boggs, Ralph S. "North Carolina White Folktales and Riddles." *JAF* 47 (1934): 289–328.

Bowman, David. "Whatever Happened to Droodles? Whatever Happened to Roger Price?" *Journal of Popular Culture* 9 (1975): 20–25.

Braddy, Haldeen. "An East Texas 'Neck' Riddle." *SFQ* 18 (1954): 222.

Brewster, Paul G. "Riddles from Southern Indiana." *SFQ* 3 (1939): 93–105.

Browne, Ray B., and Bill Brooks. "Riddles from Tippecanoe County, Indiana." *MF* 11 (1961): 155–60.

Brunvand, Jan. "More Non-Oral Riddles." *WF* 19 (1960): 132–33.

Chappell, J. W. "Riddle Me, Riddle Me, Ree." In *Folk-Say: A Regional Miscellany*, by A. B. Botkin, pp. 227–38. Norman, Okla.: University of Oklahoma Press, 1930.

Clark, Joseph D. "Riddles from North Carolina." *SFQ* 25 (1961): 113–25.

"The Conundrum." In *Tableaux, Charades and Conundrums*, Metropolitan Pamphlet Series XII, No. 4. New York: Butterick Publishing Co., 1899.

Cray, Ed. "Non-Oral Riddles." *WF* 17 (1958): 279–80.

——— and Nancy C. Leventhal. "Depth Collecting from a Sixth-Grade Class." *WF* 22 (1963): 159–63, 231–57.

Davidson, Levette J. "Some Current Folk Gestures and Signs." *American Speech* 25 (1950): 7–8.

Dirks, Martha. "Teen-Age Folklore from Kansas." *WF* 22 (1963): 89–102.

Doke, Clement M. "Lamba Folk-Lore." *MAFS* 20 (1927): 549–70.

"Elephants by the Trunk." *Time*, Aug. 2, 1963: 41.

Emrich, Duncan. "Riddle Me, Riddle Me: What Is That?" *American Heritage,* 7 (Dec. 1955): 116–19.

Evans, David. "Riddling and the Structure of Context." *JAF* 89 (1976): 166–88. A study of a riddling session in Mississippi.

Farr, T. J. "Riddles and Superstitions of Middle Tennessee." *JAF* 48 (1935): 318–36.

Fauset, Arthur H. "Folklore from Nova Scotia." *MAFS* 34 (1931): 140–76.

———. "Negro Folk Tales from the South." *JAF* 40 (1927): 213–303.

———. "Tales and Riddles Collected in Philadelphia." *JAF* 41 (1928): 529–57.

Fitzgerald, David. "Of Riddles." *The Gentlemen's Magazine* 251 (1881): 177–92.

Garrett, Allen M. "Riddles from New York State." *NCFJ* 2 (1954): 32.

Goldstein, Kenneth S. "Riddling Traditions in Northeastern Scotland." *JAF* 76 (1963): 330–36.

Georges, Robert A., and Alan Dundee. "Toward a Structural Definition of the Riddle." *JAF* 76 (1963): 111–17.

Halpert, Herbert. "The Cante Fable in Decay." *SFQ* 5 (1941): 191–200.

Hudson, Arthur P. "Some Folk Riddles from the South." *South Atlantic Quarterly* 42 (1943): 78–93.

Hull, Vernam E., and Archer Taylor. "A Collection of Welsh Riddles." *University of California Publications in Modern Philology* 26 (1942): 225–26.

Jackson, Kenneth and Edward Wilson. "The Barn Is Burning." *Folk-Lore* 47 (1936): 190–202.

Jenson, William H. "Tell Us a Riddle, But in Rhyme." *KFR* 1 (1955): 25–31.

Jordon, Philip D. "Folk Fun for English Emigrants." *SFQ* 10 (1946): 235–38.

Kelso, James A. "Riddles." In *Encyclopedia of Religion and Ethics*, James Hastings, ed., v. 10, pp. 765–70. New York: Charles Scribner's Sons, n.d.

Köngäs-Maranda, Elli. "Riddles and Riddling." *JAF* 89 (1976): 127–37.

Loomis, C. Grant. "Chain Conundrums." *WF* 7 (1948): 388.

Long, Martha. "An Old Riddle from Berkeley, California." *WF* 7 (1948): 64.

McCollum, Katherine Ann, and Kenneth W. Porter, eds. "Winter Evenings in Iowa, 1873–1880." *JAF* 56 (1943): 97–101.

"Med-O-Lark Aptitude Test." Publication of Camp Med-O-Lark, Washington, Me., Feb. 1975.

Millard, Eugenia L. "The Lore of Secret Languages." *NYFQ* 10 (1954): 103–10.

Moore, Danny W. "The Deductive Riddle: An Adaptation to Modern Society." *NCFJ* 22 (1974): 119–25.

Neal, Janice. "Wa'n't That Remarkable!" *NYFQ* 1 (1945): 209–20. New York State riddles.

Norton, F. J. "The Prisoner Who Saved His Neck with a Riddle." *Folk-Lore* 53 (1942): 27–57.

Perkins, A. E. "Riddles from Negro School-Children in New Orleans." *JAF* 35 (1922): 105–15.

Petsch, Robert, ed. "Fifty Welsh-Gypsy Folk-Riddles." *Journal of the Gypsy Lore Society* 5 (1911–1912): 251–55.

Potter, Charles F. "Riddles." In *Standard Dictionary of Folklore, Mythology, and Legend*, 2nd ed., Maria Leach, ed., pp. 939–44. New York: Funk & Wagnalls, Inc., 1972.

"The Race to Mecca." *Esquire*, Sept. 8, 1967, p. 8.

Randolph, Vance, and Mary C. Parler. "Riddles from Arkansas." *JAF* 67 (1954): 253–59.

—— and Isabel Spradley. "Ozark Mountain Riddles."

JAF 47 (1934): 81–89.

—— and Archer Taylor. "Riddles in the Ozarks." *SFQ* 8 (1944): 1–10.

Redfield, W. A. "A Collection of Middle Tennessee Riddles." *SFQ* 1 (1937): 35–50.

Roberts, Leonard. "The Cante Fable in Eastern Kentucky." *MF* 6 (1956): 69–88.

Roemer, Danielle M. "In the Eye of the Beholder: A Semiotic Analysis of the Visual Descriptive Riddle." *JAF* 95 (1982): 173–99.

Rubin, Ruth. "Some Aspects of Jewish Folksong." *NYFQ* 12 (1956): 87–95.

——. "Yiddish Riddles and Problems." *NYFQ* 12 (1956): 257–60.

Schlesinger, Marilyn R. "Riddling Questions from Los Angeles High School Students." *WF* 19 (1960): 191–95.

Taylor, Archer. "American Indian Riddles." *JAF* 57 (1944): 1–15.

——. "Problems in the Study of Riddles." *SFQ* 2 (1938): 1–9.

——. "A Punning Riddle or Jest." *WF* 22 (1963): 199.

——. "The Riddle." *CFQ* 2 (1943): 129–47.

——. "Riddles and Poetry." *SFQ* 11 (1947): 245–47.

——. "Riddles Dealing with Family Relationships." *JAF* 51 (1938): 25–37.

——. "Riddles in the Emigrants' Penny Magazine." *SFQ* 11 (1947): 139–40.

"Trade Winds." *Saturday Review of Literature*, Aug. 8, 1963, p. 7.